A a B b C c D d E e F f G g H h

The ABCs of

Environment

Bobbie Kalman

Crabtree Publishing Company

www.crabtreebooks.com

K k L l M m N n O o P p Q q R r

The ABCs of the
Natural World

Created by Bobbie Kalman

Dedicated by Kathy Middleton
To Libby, Glenn, Jordan, and Evan Little
A family that walks the walk when it comes to
caring for the environment

**Author and
Editor-in-Chief**
Bobbie Kalman

Research
Enlynne Paterson

Editor
Kathy Middleton

Proofreader
Crystal Sikkens

Design
Bobbie Kalman
Katherine Berti
Samantha Crabtree (cover)

Photo research
Bobbie Kalman
Crystal Sikkens

Production coordinator
Katherine Berti

Photographs
© Dreamstime.com: pages 8 (bottom), 11 (top)
© iStockphoto.com: page 13 (bottom)
© Shutterstock.com: cover, pages 1, 3, 4, 5,
6, 7, 8 (top and middle), 9, 10, 11 (bottom),
12, 13 (top), 14, 15, 16, 17, 18, 19, 20, 21,
22 (except middle right), 23 (oranges, mango,
lemons, coconut, and spider monkey), 24,
25, 26, 27, 28, 29 (top), 30, 31
© Wikimedia Commons: page 29 (bottom)
Other images by Comstock

Library and Archives Canada Cataloguing in Publication

Kalman, Bobbie, 1947-
    The ABCs of the environment / Bobbie Kalman.

(The ABCs of the natural world)
Includes index.
ISBN 978-0-7787-3417-8 (bound).--ISBN 978-0-7787-3437-6 (pbk.)

    1. Environmental protection--Juvenile literature. 2. Human
ecology--Juvenile literature. 3. English language--Alphabet--Juvenile
literature. I. Title. II. Series: Kalman, Bobbie, 1947- . ABCs of the
natural world.

TD170.15.K34 2009   j333.72   C2008-907903-5

Library of Congress Cataloging-in-Publication Data

Kalman, Bobbie.
    The ABCs of the environment / Bobbie Kalman.
        p. cm. -- (The ABCs of the natural world)
    Includes index.
    ISBN 978-0-7787-3437-6 (pbk. : alk. paper) -- ISBN 978-0-7787-3417-8
(reinforced library binding : alk. paper)
    1. Environmental protection--Juvenile literature. 2. Human ecology--
Juvenile literature. 3. Alphabet books--Juvenile literature. I. Title. II.
Series.

    TD170.15.K35 2009
    363.7--dc22

                                    2008052411

Crabtree Publishing Company

www.crabtreebooks.com   1-800-387-7650

**Published in Canada
Crabtree Publishing**
616 Welland Ave.
St. Catharines, Ontario
L2M 5V6

**Published in the United States
Crabtree Publishing**
PMB16A
350 Fifth Ave., Suite 3308
New York, NY 10118

**Published in the United Kingdom
Crabtree Publishing**
White Cross Mills
High Town, Lancaster
LA1 4XS

**Published in Australia
Crabtree Publishing**
386 Mt. Alexander Rd.
Ascot Vale (Melbourne)
VIC 3032

Contents

Atmosphere is air

The **atmosphere** is a blanket of air that surrounds Earth. It protects us from extreme hot and cold temperatures. The atmosphere is like a big sunscreen that **absorbs**, or takes in, most of the sun's **ultraviolet radiation** (see page 26). Without the atmosphere, there would be no life on Earth. It would be too hot during the day and too cold at night for anything to survive.

Three-quarters of the gases in Earth's atmosphere are within seven miles (11 km) of Earth's surface.

Breathe!

The atmosphere also provides the air that we need to breathe. We would not last more than a minute without air! The atmosphere contains the perfect mix of **gases** at just the right temperature to keep us alive on this planet. Air is made mainly of two gases called **nitrogen** and **oxygen**. Air also contains other gases such as **carbon dioxide** and **argon**.

*Argon is a gas that never changes or disappears. It was in the air that was once **exhaled**, or breathed out, by dinosaurs millions of years ago. The next time you take a breath, you may be **inhaling**, or breathing in, argon from a dinosaur's breath!*

Climate Change

Climate is the average weather in an area over a long period of time. Average weather includes temperature, wind, and **precipitation** such as rain or snow. Scientists believe that there has been a climate change on Earth. They call it **global warming**. This climate change is warming up Earth. It is caused by **greenhouse gases** that are created when we burn oil, natural gas, and coal. Greenhouse gases absorb heat from the sun and trap it in the atmosphere. The trapped heat then raises the temperatures on Earth.

Dangers to Earth

Even the smallest temperature changes on Earth can cause big changes in our **environment**, or natural world. It is hard for plants, animals, and even humans, to **adapt**, or get used to, these changes. Climate change causes heavier rainstorms and snowstorms, more flooding, and extreme heat in summer. Global warming may also cause **droughts**, or long periods without rain. During droughts, people and animals cannot find water, and many fires break out.

These elephants are digging for water where a river used to be. The river has dried up.

Fires break out because the land is very dry. Fires have burned forests and many homes!

There are more floods due to climate change.

In some areas, there are worse winter storms.

Earth's ecosystems

bobcat

Ecosystems are found in **habitats**. Habitats are the natural homes of plants and animals. An ecosystem also includes all the non-living parts of habitats, such as rocks, soil, water, air, and sunlight. An ecosystem is more than just a home. It is also how living things depend on one another, as well as on non-living things to stay alive.

desert tortoise

coyote

*This coyote's habitat is a **desert**. A desert is a dry area that gets very little rain. Deserts can be hot or cold. Bobcats, desert tortoises, and many kinds of snakes live in hot deserts. This desert ecosystem also includes rocks, many kinds of plants, soil, air, sunlight, and water.*

Coral reefs are warm, shallow, ocean habitats filled with fish and other creatures. Coral reefs are made up of tiny animals called **coral polyps**. There is plenty of sunlight in most coral reefs.

Forests are ecosystems with many trees and other plants. Forests also contain soil, water, air, and sunlight. These deer live in a **deciduous forest**. Deciduous trees lose their leaves in autumn and grow them back in spring. Learn about other forests on page 23.

Footprints on Earth

A **carbon footprint** is the measure of how much carbon dioxide a person creates by using electricity, gasoline, and oil. Bigger amounts of greenhouse gases, such as carbon dioxide, are causing global warming. We leave smaller carbon footprints when we use less heat, electricity, and gasoline, because we cause less damage to Earth. Eating less beef is another way to reduce our carbon footprints. Raising beef cattle is the main reason that **rain forests** are being cut down (see page 23). Rain forests clean the air. Cows also create greenhouse gas through their waste and the gas they pass.

Try to walk lightly on Earth. What can you do to leave a smaller footprint?

Pretend you are following yourself around and become aware of your footprint. How much energy do you waste? How many hamburgers do you eat each week?

Green goodness

One way to reduce your carbon footprint is to eat more Earth-friendly foods. How far has the food you eat traveled? Many foods are **transported** in trucks, trains, or by ship. Transporting food adds a lot to your footprint because the vehicles burn gasoline and oil, which create greenhouse gases. You can reduce your footprint by buying foods that were grown close to home. You can even grow some yourself!

Many farms allow you to pick your own fruits and vegetables.

*Ask your parents to shop for fruits and vegetables that were grown **locally**, or near your home. They are fresher and better for your health, as well.*

Habitat loss

What would you do if someone took over your home and moved in? You would have to find somewhere else to live. What if you could not find the right kind of home or the right kind of food to keep you alive? Plants and animals are dying because they are losing their homes and food to human beings. When human beings build roads, cities, and farms, they destroy the natural habitats of plants and animals. Losing homes in nature is called **habitat loss**.

When people cut down forests, many kinds of animals are left without food or places to live.

12

Endangered animals

Endangered animals are in danger of becoming **extinct**, or disappearing from Earth forever (see pages 28-29). Habitat loss is the biggest reason that animals become endangered. Elephants, tigers, leopards, and monkeys are all endangered for this reason.

Douc langurs are monkeys that live in the forests of Vietnam and Laos, which are countries in Asia. These colorful monkeys are endangered because of habitat loss.

*When animals cannot find enough food to eat, they look for food on people's farms. Some farmers put up electric fences to keep out wild animals such as elephants. The fences give **shocks** to the animals that come close. A shock is a painful jolt of electricity. This young elephant is trying to grab some grass from the other side of an electric fence.*

13

Interconnected!

All living things are **interconnected**, or joined to one another. What we do to one part of Earth makes a difference to all its other parts. Nature takes care of us. Nature needs us to take care of it, too. All life is **interdependent**. Interdependent means that each part needs every other part. Everything you eat, breathe, drink, and use comes from Earth. Air, water, sunshine, plants, animals, people, rocks, and soil are part of Earth, and they are parts of you.

Plants use sunshine, air, and water to make food. We eat plants. Animals eat plants, too.

Plants make the air fresh for us to breathe.

Earth gives us water to drink. We need to keep the water on Earth clean.

We are all connected to Earth and to one another!

We are connected to the animals on Earth, too. We need to help them stay alive.

Jump for joy!

Joy is a feeling of great happiness. We spend a lot of time indoors, and sometimes we forget that we are a part of the natural world. Spending time in nature makes us feel great. Enjoy the fresh air and jump for joy under the sun!

Share the joy and beauty of nature by painting a picture of the great outdoors!

16

Kindness and Love

Kindness is showing that we care. We cannot change all the things that are wrong with the environment, but even small changes can make a big difference! With your friends, make a plan to show your love for Earth. When you show your love for your natural home, others will want to do it, too. Good feelings spread quickly!

Plant trees in your yard or community. Planting trees helps clean the air.

Melting mountains

The Earth is getting warmer, and the ice around the world is melting faster than usual. The **glaciers** at the North Pole and South Pole are melting. Glaciers are slow-moving rivers of ice. The glaciers on many high mountains, such as the Himalaya mountains and Mount Kilimanjaro, are melting very fast, too. Ice helps keep Earth cool. It reflects the sun's rays and cools the air. As glaciers get smaller, the Earth gets warmer. As Earth gets warmer, more ice melts.

glacier

The glaciers on Mount Kilimanjaro in Africa may be gone by the year 2020.

Natural resources

Anything we use from nature is a **natural resource**. Water, air, sunlight, wood, oil, and minerals are examples of natural resources. There are two types of natural resources—**renewable** and **non-renewable**. Renewable resources are sunlight, air, and water. Plants and animals are renewable, too, but they take time to grow. Oil and minerals are non-renewable. These resources took millions of years to form, and once we use them up, they are gone. We can protect our natural resources by keeping them clean and not using them too quickly.

Plants take time to grow.

This girl had to walk a long way to find water!

(left) The air we breathe may not be clean or healthy. This girl is wearing a mask because the air in her city is very dirty.

*Oil is a non-renewable resource. These machines, called **rocking chairs**, are taking oil from the ground.*

Oceans on Earth

Three-quarters of Earth is covered by oceans. Earth's five oceans are the Pacific, Atlantic, Indian, Arctic, and Southern oceans. Oceans are in trouble. The biggest environmental problems for oceans are **overfishing**, rising water levels, and **pollution**. Overfishing is taking too many fish from the ocean. When too many fish are caught, there is not enough food left for bigger fish and other ocean animals to eat. These animals then starve. Melting glaciers are adding water to oceans, causing higher water levels. Many people who live near oceans are getting more rain and bigger storms. Polar bears are becoming endangered because their icy ocean habitat is melting.

*This polar bear is floating on a small ice **floe**, a piece of ice that was once part of a huge glacier. Polar bears hunt seals in the ocean and drag them onto ice to eat them. When glacier ice melts, polar bears cannot eat the animals they hunt. Many bears are starving. If they cannot find new sources of food, polar bears will soon become extinct.*

P p P p P p P p P p P p P p P p P

Pollution

Pollution is putting harmful substances into the air, water, and soil. Almost all of the Earth's pollution is human-made waste. When we pollute the environment, we are polluting ourselves. We breathe dirty air. We drink dirty water. We eat food that grows in polluted soil or water. If the air, water, and soil are not healthy, how can we stay healthy?

inhaler

*This boy has **asthma**. Asthma makes it hard to breathe, so he is using an inhaler to help. Pollution makes asthma even worse.*

These dead fish are on the beach of an ocean. The fish have died from pollution. Chemicals that are dumped into oceans cause pollution.

Quiz questions

How well do you know the environment? Find out by matching these questions to the answers in the pictures!

1. What does interconnected mean?
2. What are rivers of ice called?
3. What is a long time without rain called?
4. What are the natural homes of plants and animals called?
5. Which animals create a lot of greenhouse gas?
6. What is the biggest threat to animals in the wild?
7. Which natural resources would you find at a beach?
8. What uses carbon dioxide?
9. What is dirty air or water called?

polluted

glaciers

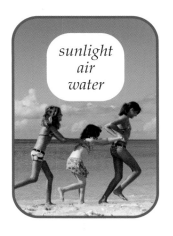

*sunlight
air
water*

habitats

habitat loss

plants

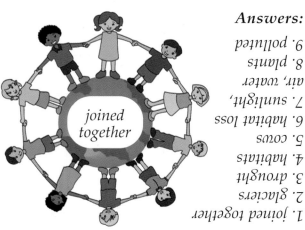

joined together

Answers:

9. *polluted*
8. *plants*
7. *sunlight, air, water*
6. *habitat loss*
5. *cows*
4. *habitats*
3. *drought*
2. *glaciers*
1. *joined together*

drought

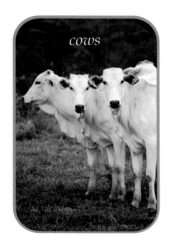

cows

Rain forests

Rain forests are called "the lungs of Earth." They clean the air by absorbing, or taking in, large amounts of carbon dioxide and by making oxygen, which people and animals need. Rain forests are home to more than half of the world's **species**, or types, of plants and animals.

Cut down!

Rain forests are quickly disappearing, however. They are being cut down for wood and to make room for soy and cattle farming. Each day, over 100 rainforest plant and animal species are becoming extinct. The people who live in rain forests are disappearing, too. Some have been forced to leave their homes and land.

Spider monkeys live in rain forests. They are losing more and more of their habitats.

These and many more foods were first found in rain forests.

oranges

mangoes

lemons

coconuts

peanuts

pineapples

eggplant

onions

sugar

corn

23

Solar energy

Solar energy is energy from the sun. We get more energy from the sun in one hour than the amount of energy the whole world uses in one year! When the sun shines through your window and makes your room warm, you are using solar energy. When you hang your clothes out to dry, you are using solar energy. Solar panels on the roofs of houses absorb the energy from the sun and turn it into electricity. Solar panels are known as **photovoltaics**. Solar panels cost money to buy, but the sun's energy is free!

solar panel

(left) This home has many solar panels on its roof. The home is heated by free energy from the sun.

*(below) Wind power is also solar energy because the sun's energy creates the weather that makes wind. Wind turns the propellers. The propellers drive a **generator**. The generator makes electricity.*

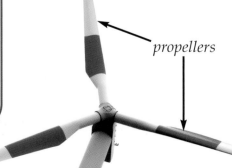

propellers

Think three!

Three simple words remind us to think about how we can help the environment. They are the Three Rs—**reduce**, **reuse**, and **recycle**. To reduce means to use less of something such as water or gas. It also means buying fewer things.

- *Turn off the water when you brush your teeth.*
- *Take quick showers.*
- *Turn down the heat and wear a sweater.*
- *Turn off lights when you are not in a room.*

Reuse

To reuse means to use things over again or to find new uses for them. Instead of throwing away old toys or books, trade them for toys or books your friends no longer want. Their toys will be new to you!

Buying clothes at second-hand stores is a great way to reuse and save money!

Recycle

To recycle is to change old materials into new materials that can be used again. Most places have recycling programs to reduce waste. Almost everything we throw away can be recycled.

*Recycle paper, plastic, and aluminum. Put food scraps into a **compost** bin.*

UV radiation

UV or ultraviolet radiation is a harmful part of sunlight that can cause skin to burn. It can also damage plants and animals. The **ozone layer** protects us from most of the sun's ultraviolet radiation. This layer of gases, ten to thirty miles (16 to 50 kms) above Earth's surface, acts like a big sunscreen. Unfortunately, the ozone layer is thinning, and there is even a hole in it above the continent of Antarctica.

When you go outdoors, you should wear a hat and sunglasses. You also need to put sunscreen on your skin.

UV radiation is dangerous to frogs, such as the poison dart frog above. Frogs have thin skin, and they cannot wear sunscreen. UV radiation can make frogs sick and even kill them. It also kills the eggs of frogs. The dead frog below has been dried out by the sun's UV rays.

Water planet

All living things need water to survive. Almost three-quarters of our bodies are water. Almost three-quarters of our planet is water, too, but most of the water is too salty to drink. Few of us think about water. We turn on the tap, and water flows out, but billions of people on Earth do not have clean water to drink.

This African village is lucky to have a well. Many people have to walk for hours to find water.

eXtinct is forever!

Extinct means gone forever. Thousands of species of animals are in danger of disappearing from Earth forever. When an animal becomes extinct, we will never see it again. Many endangered animals are at risk of becoming extinct. Some are already extinct in the **wild**. The wild is places that are not controlled by people. Many people are helping endangered animals. You can help, too, by raising money for a **conservation** group such as World Wildlife Fund or Friends of the Island Fox (see next page).

This baby monkey is a golden lion tamarin. It is endangered because the trees in its rainforest habitat are being cut down. There are very few of these monkeys left in the wild.

Not all endangered animals are on land. There are many endangered animals in oceans, too. Sea turtles live in oceans. All sea turtles are endangered, but hawksbill sea turtles are more endangered than some other turtles. Some people hunt these sea turtles for their beautiful shells.

Back into the wild!

Island foxes live in the Channel Islands near Southern California. About five years ago, there were fewer than 100 foxes left on all the islands. People then captured and protected them so they could have babies. Now there are about 650 foxes, and they have gone back into their wild habitats. Their story shows that people can help endangered animals! Find out how you can help by logging on to this Internet address: http://islandfox.org

Island foxes are small foxes that are about the size of cats.

Y y Y y Y y Y y Y y Y y Y y Y y Y y Y y Y y Y

Yes, you can do it!

Eat fresh food. It is better for you and for the environment!

There are many ways that you can help the environment. Here are just a few easy changes you can make. You can do it—yes, you can!

Ask your parents to use cloth bags for groceries.

*Take your old computers to an **e-cycling** plant.*

Wear a sweater instead of turning up the heat at home.

Drink filtered tap water. Bottled water creates waste.

Remember that Earth is your home! Spend more time outdoors and feel your connection to the natural world!

ZzZzZzZzZzZzZzZzZzZzZz

Zero emission

Zero emission is an engine, motor, or other energy source, that **emits**, or puts out, no waste products that pollute air or water or change the climate. Your bicycle is a zero-emission vehicle. Scientists are working on new kinds of cars and energy sources that will not add dangerous greenhouse gases to the air.

Will you drive a car like this when you grow up?

AaBbCcDdEeFfGgHh

Glossary

Note: Some boldfaced words are defined where they appear in the book.

compost Plant or food waste that can be added to soil to help plants grow

conservation Protecting and saving nature and wildlife

e-cycling Recycling electronics

environment The natural world, including the changes that humans have made to it

global warming The steady rise of the temperature on Earth

greenhouse gases Gases such as carbon dioxide that trap heat within the Earth's atmosphere

ozone layer A layer of gases that protects living things from the sun's ultraviolet radiation

pollution A substance that makes the environment dirty or destroys it

rain forest A forest found in warm parts of Earth, which receives over 80 inches (200 cm) of rain each year

renewable Able to be replaced

resource Something valuable

species A group of closely related living things that can make babies

transport To carry something from one place to another

Index

Printed in the U.S.A. - CG